SCOTTISH RAILWAYS
in the heyday of steam

SCOTTISH RAILWAYS

in the heyday of steam

H. C. CASSERLEY

D. BRADFORD BARTON LTD

Frontispiece: 'The Northern Belle' on Glenfinnan Viaduct on the Mallaig line in June 1934, hauled by two 'Glens', the leading one being No.9496 *Glen Moidart.* This was an ambitious scheme launched by the L.N.E.R. in 1933, comprising a week's tour of Scotland from London in a train with full facilities, including sleeping car accommodation—in fact, a mobile hotel in which participants lived for the whole seven days. It was repeated in 1934, but never again; later tours of a similar nature were mostly organised privately during the later 1950s and early 1960s, but arranged with overnight conventional hotel accommodation (see page 90). [Colling Turner]

© Copyright D. Bradford Barton Ltd ISBN 085153 3507

Published by Lomond Books
36 West Shore Road, Granton, Edinburgh EH5 1QD

Printed and bound in Great Britain by BPC Hazell Books Ltd

introduction

Which period of British railway history may be regarded as the 'heyday of steam operation' is to some extent a debatable point. Possibly the years between the wars, the 1930s in particular—the days of such exploits as 'The Royal Scot', 'Flying Scotsman', 'Cheltenham Flyer', 'Silver Jubilee', 'Coronation' and other outstanding activities—might well lay claim to such distinction. Some might even opt for the colourful pre-Grouping days before World War I.

On the other hand, what of the post-second World War era, commencing with Nationalisation on 1 July 1948, and the new British Railways organisation. This body confidently expressed its faith in the continuance of steam haulage for main line work, concentrating on twelve standard designs to cover requirements for the foreseeable future. In all, nearly 1000 steam locomotives (999 to be exact) were built before the sudden reversal of policy under which steam was to be entirely phased out by 1975—in the event such was the hurry to implement the programme that it was actually completed by 1968, so much was the sudden prejudice against steam in favour of diesel or electric haulage.

Perhaps I might put forward a third alternative with which some may disagree, that the first half of the 1950s—those last years before the dieselisation programme was inaugurated and before it got well under way—was, looking back in retrospect, one of the most interesting periods of all. It is difficult to realise that it was at this time still possible to travel, outside the electrified areas, the length and breadth of Great Britain almost entirely by steam, apart from a few experimental diesel-electrics such as L.M.S. Nos.10000 and 10001, the Western Region gas turbine and their early diesel railcars, and one or two other miscellaneous oddments.

So far as Scotland is concerned it was still at this period 100 per cent steam. The rapid encroachment of diesel multiple units very quickly changed the scene so far as branch line and cross country services were concerned. Up to that time one could still make a local journey behind a perhaps elderly steam locomotive and maybe coaches of equal vintage, old but certainly more pleasant and comfortable than the new diesel multiple unit railcars with their noise, smell and vibration—all introduced in the sacred name of 'progress'. Of course, they were cheaper to run, but with it, much less reliable.

These years leading up to what was so quickly to transform the entire scene—not of course the later deplorable running down period of the 1960s—must surely come within the concept of the Heyday of Steam. This volume is designed therefore to cover broadly these two periods pre- and post-war, and the illustrations are divided fairly evenly between them, with a few of special interest to depict the last stages, mainly the work of that fine photographer of recent years, Derek Cross, through the courtesy of whom I have been able to fill in some areas and subjects somewhat deficient in my own collection.

The majority of the photographs, especially the earlier ones, are of my own taking, but a few others of pre-war days have been used, duly acknowledged where the authorship is known. This is not always the case and my apologies are due to any of my older contemporaries whose work has been necessarily used without previous consultation.

H.C. Casserley

Carlisle is often regarded as the gateway to Scotland, but it is of course in what is now known as Cumbria. The actual border is at Gretna, scene of many runaway marriages in the past when the matrimonial laws of Scotland were more favourable for runaway couples. This view, taken on 14 May 1936, shows an up Scottish express to London hauled by a then unrebuilt 'Scot' No.6113 *Cameronian*.

There were two stations at Gretna. The first, the Caledonian, right on the border, is seen here, with the junction of the Glasgow & South Western line branching off to the left in the background; Jubilee No.5623 *Palestine*, with an up local on the same date as above.

The Glasgow & South Western station at Gretna Green, well inside the border in Dumfriesshire. Fowler Class 2 4-4-0 is in charge of an up mixed train on 14 May 1936.

Another view of Gretna Green, with compound No.1180, rather unusually for that time working an express freight. These engines had been introduced for main line working in Scotland, which they performed with outstanding success for many years. Both stations are now closed; Gretna Green lost its passenger service in December 1965 and Gretna in September 1951.

A more recent view, taken near Southwick, on the main line between Dumfries and Stranraer Harbour, over which Irish boat trains for England ran in connection with steamer sailings to Larne. Since closure of the line in 1965—a Beeching casualty—they have had to be diverted by a more circuitous route. The section of the line between Castle Douglas and Portpatrick was a joint concern, known as the Portpatrick & Wigtownshire, owned by the L.N.W.R. and Midland, Caledonian, and Glasgow & South Western, one of the largest of all jointly-owned lines, with a route mileage of 82 miles. It was the only instance of any Scottish railway being owned, or partly owned, by an English Company.

May 1965, when a series of Sunday troop trains was run, was the last blaze of glory for the 'Port' line, due to be closed five months later. One of them is seen here passing the secret Ordnance factory built at Southwick during the war, which had an intensive internal railway system, relics of which are seen in the background. This view, taken on 16 May 1965, shows a Stranraer—Woodburn troop special hauled by No.72008 *Clan Macleod,* one of the twelve standard designs built in 1952 under the original BR standard types programme. It was a light-weight version of the better known 'Britannias', in this case designed specially for use in Scotland, but of which only ten examples appeared. They had necessarily short lives, and all were scrapped between 1962-66.

[Derek Cross]

A scene on the Whithorn branch, which left the main line of the Portpatrick & Wigtownshire at Newton Stewart, running to a terminus on a southern promontory of the county of Wigtown. The morning pick-up goods train near Whauphill, 26 April 1963, is headed by L.M.S. type Class 2 lightweight 2-6-0 No.46467, built in 1951.   [Derek Cross]

Dumfries to Kirkcudbright local near Tarff on 11 July 1963, hauled by standard L.M.S. Fairburn 2-6-4T 42689. This ranch, like the main Wigtownshire line, was completely closed on 14 June 1965.   [M. Mensing]

ranraer Harbour, 21 June 1937, with a boat train about to leave behind Class 2 4-4-0 No.646 and rwich 2-6-0 No.2918.

The ubiquitous L.M.S. 'Black 5s' were used extensively in Scotland, as elsewhere, and this impressive photograph shows No.44977, piloted by one of its B.R. successors, No.73145, pausing at Girvan on 30 June with a train for Stranraer before tackling the stiff 1 in 54 ascent to Pinmore summit.   [Derek Cross]

A Whitehall–Ayr train at Annbank Junction amid the busy coalfields of Ayrshire, where lie some of th largest deposits of coal in Scotland, 22 June 1962. L.M.S. Class 4 No.44189 was one of a batch built i 1925 at the St. Rollox works of the Caledonian Railway, mainly for use in Scotland.   [Derek Cross

12

Jubilee No.45728 *Defiance* with a Stranraer–Glasgow train, running into the lonely station at Glenwhilly on 2 July 1957 about midway on an ascent of several miles over the moorlands with a gradient of between 1 in 57 and 1 in 100. This remote station was completely closed in September 1965.

Snow is an ever present hazard in Scotland, particularly on the Highland, but in March 1965 one of the worst blizzards within living memory hit the south-west of the country, which normally escapes the extremes of such weather. This Girvan–Glasgow train seen at Maybole on 5 March 1965 would normally at this period have been a DMU, but these contraptions were quite unable to cope with such conditions, where between Ayr and Girvan the cuttings were deep in snow, and a steam train had to be substituted headed by B.R. Standard Class 4 2-6-0 No.76096.

[Derek Cross]

14

Another impressive view taken in similar conditions—Jubilee No.45588 *Kashmir* running northbound 'light engine' near Barrhill, on 18 February 1963. After a blizzard on 15 February, Stranraer was cut off for three days and once the line was opened a heavy goods was worked through from Ayr, piloted from Girvan by Stranraer's regular 'Paddy' engine (a nickname for the Irish Mail loco) seen here near Barrhill over the newly ploughed-out line.

[Derek Cross]

An Ardrossan to Darvel train on the last passenger working over that branch, 4 June 1964, at Crosshouse Junction. B.R. Standard Class 3 2-6-0 No.77016 was one of only twenty of this class built, divided equally between the Scottish and North Eastern Regions. They were never seen in the south except for one, No.77014, which ended its days on the Southern in 1966/67. [Derek Cross]

16

L.M.S. Fowler Class 2 4-4-0 No.40590 with the Ayr–Dalmellington train near Dalrymple, August 1958. This branch was entirely closed in April 1964. [Derek Cross]

Black 5 No.45456 leaving Drumlanrig Tunnel on the G. & S.W.R. main line between Glasgow and Carlisle near Carronbridge, with a down freight on 10 July 1963. [M. Mensing]

On the Nith Valley line, rebuilt 'Scot' No.46107, *Argyll & Sutherland Highlander,* was photographed on 14 April 1962 most unusually working a local from Glasgow to Carlisle.   [Derek Cross]

A Newcastle–Arrochar excursion hauled by 'Britannia' No.70038 *Robin Hood* photographed in the Clyde Valley near Lamington, 26 May 1964.
[Derek Cross]

With the mountainous nature of the country, Scotland's railways abound in severe gradients. One of the best known, and among the most taxing to be found on any main trunk route in the British Isles, was that at Beattock on the Caledonian main line between Carlisle and Glasgow. With a continuous ascent of ten miles up gradients between 1 in 74 and 1 in 88, it was necessary in steam days for all but the lightest trains to be provided with banking assistance. This view, taken on 1 June 1951, shows C.R. 0-4-4T No.55237, one of four specially fitted with strengthened front buffer beams, giving assistance to a north-bound express. On the right can be seen the Moffat branch train, here worked by a steam pull-and-push unit, never very widely used in Scotland.

'The Royal Scot' on the bank on the same date, hauled by Stanier Pacific No.46232 *Duchess of Montrose*.

another view on Beattock, also on 1 June 1951, in this case of a freight banked by C.R. 4-6-2T No.55361.

A rarity north of the Border, the Class 9 2-10-0 were B.R.'s final steam design, and the last to be built in 1960 was the end of the reign of a long line of steam locomotives. Ten of them, Nos.92020-92029 constructed in 1953, were experimentally fitted with Franco Crosti twin boilers. One of these, No.92024, is seen leaving the Greskine passing loop halfway up the bank, on 25 July 1964. It will be noted that it is carrying a 12A shed plate (Carlisle Kingmoor), apparently a temporary transfer, which accounts for its presence in this unusual location. These ten engines normally spent their working lives in the south, based on Wellingborough, and were rarely seen even in the northern parts of England, let alone penetrating north of the Border. Nor for that matter did their much more numerous conventional sisters. [Derek Cross]

e much more numerous 2-8-0 W.D. engines, no less than 733 in all, were to be found in all Regions, and No.90152 seen here, at Beattock station starting a vigorous ascent from the foot of the bank.

Caledonian 0-4-4T No.55124 crossing Coulter Viaduct on the Symington–Peebles branch, 30 September 1961. This was on the occasion of a special railtour, as the branch had lost its passenger service in June 1950, although it remained open as far as Broughton for freight until 1966. [Derek Cross]

A southbound goods from Millerhill to Carlisle via the Waverley Route passing Lady Victoria colliery near Newtongrange, 3 July 1965, behind L.M.S. 'Black Five' No.45254. This was the erstwhile North British route between Edinburgh and Carlisle, which was closed in January 1969, having the unenviable distinction of being the first Scottish main line to be completely abandoned. [Derek Cross] ·

L.M.S. Compounds were introduced to Scotland in the early years of the grouping and quickly establis_ themselves under the capable hands of the Scottish drivers as being able to undertake top link work on b the C.R. and G. & S.W.R. main lines, perhaps in an even greater degree than on their native Midland syst It was not unknown for them to be seen tackling trains of twelve or more coaches single-handed. No._ is seen here at Annan in 1927 with a main line express piloting G. & S.W.R. 4-6-0 No.14672—a type wh they were very soon to displace.

No.1139 working a Carlisle—Glasgow express, entering Carstairs on 4 August 1

Glasgow (St.Enoch)—now closed—
was a lively place in its heyday an
up to the early 1930s a variety of
several classes of G. & S.W.R.
4-4-0s could be seen working the
busy service of main and semi
main line trains into Renfrew and
Ayrshire and other destinations.
They were very soon to be
displaced by Fowler Class 2
4-4-0s, one of which is seen in
the background of this illustratio
of No.14117, taken on 11 Augus
1930.

One of Whitelegg's very fine
series of six 4-6-4 tanks, No.154(
leaving St.Enoch with a train of
six wheelers in June 1928.
[W.H. Whitwor

No.14375, another and larger variety of G. & S.W.R. 4-4-0, photographed on 11 June 1927. Of the major pre-grouping railways which came into the L.M.S. orbit at the grouping, the Glasgow & South Western fared the worst. All the passenger engines had gone well before 1939 and hardly any others survived the war.

The L.M.S. Class 2s formed an essential part of the scene at St. Enoch for many years, and No.40620 is seen here on 9 August 1961 with a train for Kilmacolm during their declining years before total replacement by diesel railcars. As far as this station is concerned, complete closure took place in 1966-7, when all the traffic was transferred to the neighbouring Central station of the Caledonian.

30 Caledonian McIntosh 0-4-4T No.55228 leaving Central on 23 April 1948 with a train around the Cathcart Circle serving some of the outer suburbs of the city; it would arrive back again after a journey of about half an hour. These trains were sometimes worked by main line engines, working tender first after arrival with an express after replenishing water supplies. This would result in their being in a position to take out another train over the main line without the additional necessity of turning.

Glasgow Central, the Caledonian's principal station and one of the four of the city's main line terminals—now reduced to two—was a busy and fascinating place, with continuing arrivals and departures of both main line as well as a busy suburban service, all entirely steam worked until the late 1950s. This is a typical view of a local train leaving on 24 April 1948 behind a recently built Fairburn 2-6-4T, No.2242.

Mount Florida, a typical station on the Cathcart Circle, in July 1957, with B.R. Standard 2-6-4T No.800 working a Central to Central train.

There was also a low-level station at Glasgow Central, steam worked, and as this underground line was for the most part in tunnel it was subject to smoke and fumes which must have been on a par with the old Metropolitan in London before that system was electrified in 1905. In this case moreover, the locomotives were not even fitted with condensing apparatus. This view, taken on 10 September 1955, shows a train with 2-6-2T No.40187. The line was closed in October 1964 but there are plans to re-open it—using electric traction.

The central section of the low level line, in the heart of the city, was entirely in tunnel, whereas on the outskirts it emerged into the open. This scene is of the southern terminus at Rutherglen, with its station adjacent to one on the main line to Carstairs and the south. 2-6-2T No.40188 and other engines are visible, 20 June 1960.

Another view on the Glasgow underground line, most of which was constructed on the cut-and-cover principle and at this point leaving a small gap open to the skies between the tunnel and the platform. This train is from Possil to Rutherglen, entering Stobcross on 5 July 1957 with 2-6-4T No.42165.

The North British also had its below-surface railway with a low level platform at its principal station at Glasgow (Queen Street). This line however, although much of it was in tunnel along the central section, had rather more open sections, and consequently did not suffer so much from a smoke problem. This view, taken on 11 August 1930 at Charing Cross shows Gresley G.N.R. type N2 0-6-2T No.4736 with a train on one of the several radiating services out of the city which used the central section, in this case one to Caldercruix, on the Edinburgh via Bathgate line. This no longer carries a passenger service and the trains which still remain in operation are now electrically operated.

Sunshine and shadow at Queen Street High Level station, 24 April 1948, showing one of the Robinson G.C.R.-ty 'Director' Class 4-4-0s built by Gresley in 1924 especially for use in Scotland. These appropriately bore Scottish nam this one being B.R. 62677 *Edie Ochiltree*.

Another view at Queen Street, with A4 No.60012 *Commonwealth of Australia* about to head into the tunnel and the famous Cowlairs bank, 18 February 1950.

Falahill, eighteen miles out of Edinburgh on the now-closed 'Waverley' route (see also page 26) was the summit of a nine mile hard slog, mainly at 1 in 70. As previously mentioned, this route was entirely closed in January 1969. V2 No.60933 heads a southbound freight, 25 May 1962.   [Derek Cross]

A view on Cowlairs bank itself, with A3 No.2508 *Brown Jack* with an express for Edinburgh, 26 October 1945.

The rear view of the same train on the 1 in 41 section of Cowlairs bank. In earlier years trains here were assisted by rope haulage, but since about the turn of the century banking engines were employed, usually a N.B.R. 0-6-2T—in this case No.9858.

Newly-constructed Thompson B1s at Edinburgh (Waverley) in the early days of Nationalisation, 24 April 194: No.E1292 (above) with temporary B.R. number, stands at the main up platform with a southbound express. No.6130 (below) is in L.N.E.R. apple-green livery and with number on the buffer beam before the introduction of smoke bo door number plates. This train is in one of the northern platforms, probably destined for Dundee.

The well-known view of the railway in Princes Street Gardens at Edinburgh, surmounted by the famous castle. Numerous photographs have been taken in this picturesque setting, typified by this view of the 'Queen of Scots' Pullman car train in August 1929 headed by North British 'Atlantic' No.9877 *Liddesdale*.   [Colling Turner]

N.B.R. 0-6-0T
No. 8477, one of the
station pilots at
Edinburgh (Waverley)
on 24 April 1948.
During the last
year or two before
Nationalisation, the
L.N.E.R. had adopted
the policy of painting
shunting engines
permanently used on
such duties—and
consequently much in
the public eye—in fully
lined out passenger
green livery. They
were also kept in tip-
top clean condition.

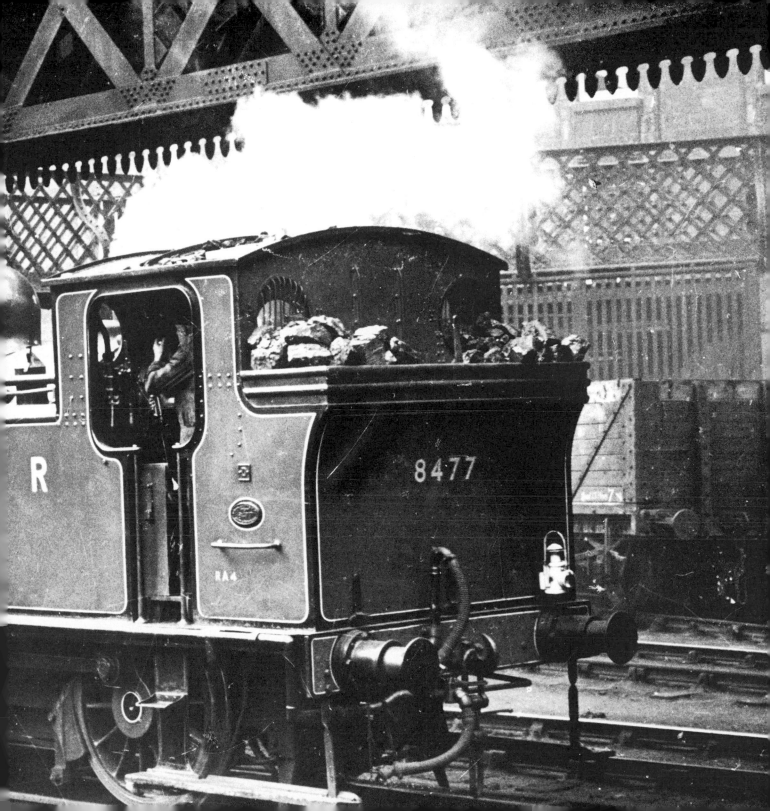

Gresley's experimental 'hush-hush' 4-6-4 No.10000, photographed in its original condition, probably around 1929 the year of its construction. Apparently it is undergoing trials, as suggested by the recording apparatus mounted on the side of the engine, whilst the leading coach appears to be a dynamometer car.

North Queensferry, at the northern end of the Forth Bridge, 12 April 1946, showing a local train for Edinburgh hauled by Gresley V1 2-6-2T No.2915. This station was replaced by a completely new one in 1954.

Photographs of the Forth Bridge have been taken over the years in countless numbers. This famous structure is represented here by two interesting views. Below is a freight headed by N.B.R. 4-4-0 No.9278 *Glen Lyon* in June 1929.

The four generations of Caledonian 'Dunalastairs' introduced by McIntosh in 1897 were generally regarded as amongst the foremost express engines of their day. They performed hard work as top-link expresses for many years right through to the earlier days of the grouping. No.14458 is seen here during the later 1920s leaving Perth with an Aberdeen express.

Gresley's three-cylinder 4-4-0s of the 'Shire' and 'Hunt' classes introduced in 1927 were confined almost entirely to the Scottish and North Eastern areas. No.62714 *Perthshire* is seen here running into Perth on 18 June 1949 with a train from Edinburgh.

Highland Railway; the overnight 'Royal Highlander' from Euston seen leaving Perth at 6.30 a.m. on 22 May 1928, with Nos.14693 *Foulis Castle* and 14675 *Taymouth Castle*.

A Glasgow–Aberdeen express passing Dunblane, 2 March 1963, headed by A3 No.60090 *Grand Parade.* It was something of an anomaly that the last years of steam on this former Caledonian route should have been largely monopolised by L.N.E.R. Pacifics already displaced by diesels from their normal habitat.

[Derek Cross]

In the opposite direction, an up Aberdeen–Glasgow express runs through Dunblane station on 29 July 1964, with A4 No.60007 *Sir Nigel Gresley*. During this period A2s and A4s were the staple diet for these services, the A3 illustrated opposite being relatively uncommon.   [Derek Cross]

In the late 1930s some of the 'Clan' class 4-6-0s from the Highland were transferred to Glasgow for working over the Oban Road, where they were found eminently suitable, although in later years they were inevitably replaced by Black Fives. No.14765 *Clan Stewart* is seen here at Stirling on 20 June 1937.

In an attempt to minimise operating costs of branch lines the L.N.E.R. acquired in the 1930s considerable numbers of Sentinel railcars, and a few were allocated to Scotland. Imaginatively, they were all named after famous stage coaches of the past including No.32 *Fair Maid* photographed at Alloa on 19 July 1931 with the branch service to Alva.

Branch line steam in its last phase; as late as 1955 one could still travel on secondary routes in such trains as these two; illustrated above is a Dundee to Thornton Junction train behind N.B.R. 'Scott' class 4-4-0 No.62418 *The Pirate*, seen at St. Andrews on 8 September of that year. Below is a train about to cross Lochearnhead viaduct on 2 June 1951 behind Caledonian Dunalastair No.54476. Nowadays such journeys, if possible at all, would be in the inevitable diesel multiple unit; in these particular cases, however, both the lines have been entirely closed, in January 1969 and October 1951 respectively.

The Tay Bridge is well known by the story of the disaster to the original structure in 1879. This scene is on the central span of the 'new' bridge, taken on 3 October 1946, with an up freight headed by Gresley A3 Pacific No.57 *Ormonde*.

A freight with WD 2-8-0 No.78668, 5 October 1946, at the southern end of the bridge.

This most original and impressive view of the Tay Bridge, from the Dundee side, is of unknown origin and date, but is thought to have been taken about 1935, with a train hauled by a North British 4-4-0.

On the steep ascent at 1 in 66 from Dundee station to the Bridge. L.M.S. 2-8-0 No.8504, assisted by N.B.R. 0-6-0s Nos.9208 (old number) and 4634 (new number), 3 October 1946.

The Great North of Scotland was the smallest of the five principal Scottish railways, and ran a smart and efficient service within the confines of its virtually exclusive area, comprising a large proportion of the county of Aberdeenshire, with some incursion into Morayshire, but it never succeeded in its ambition to reach Inverness, capital of the Highlands. Its most southerly branch was the 43¼ mile one from Aberdeen to Ballater, usually known as the Deeside line, over which many royal specials ran in the past when the members of the Royal family were in residence at Balmoral Castle. Regrettably the line was completely closed in the 1960s, along with many other branches, and today virtually all that remains of the old G.N.oS. system is the main line from Aberdeen to Keith, which still forms part of the important inter-city route to Inverness, together with the branch to Fraserburgh, still in use for goods traffic. This view, taken on 16 June 1949, shows a down Deeside line train not far out of Aberdeen, hauled by No.62276 *Andrew Bain,* one of the last of many classes of 4-4-0, this being the largest type used by the G.NoS.R.

The up 'Granite City' express leaving Aberdeen on 16 June 1949, with compound No.40923 piloting Black Five No.44997. Below; The up 'Aberdonian' on the same day with rebuilt A2 Pacific No.60502 *Earl Marischal*. These two views reflect the last vestige of the old rivalry between the East and West Coast routes between London and Aberdeen, at its height during the famous races of 1888 and 1895. The winner would be the first to reach Kinnaber Junction, where the C.R. and N.B.R. routes converged, the last 38 miles into Aberdeen being over the same tracks (owned by the Caledonian) and over the last section depicted in these photographs, into Aberdeen itself.

After the Grouping, the L.N.E.R. introduced the 4-6-0 to the G.N.oS.R. for the first time by sending some Great Eastern Holden 4-6-0s up north to help out with the principal main line workings, although the 4-4-0s continued to hold their own alongside these new importations. This view, also taken on 16 June 1949, shows one of these, No.61552, on an up Deeside train approaching Ferryhill Junction where the branch joined the main C.R. line from the south.

Kittybrewster on 17 June 1949 G.N.oS.R. No.62270 is visible, whilst on the right can be seen another of the 0-4-2Ts, No.68193.

G.N.oS.R. 0-4-2T
No.8191, one of four
used for shunting on
the quayside at
Aberdeen Harbour,
16 October 1947.
These lines were
served by a branch from
the main line at
Kittybrewster, where
the principal shed and
workshops of the
G.N.oS.R. were
situated, down to the
waterside at the
original terminus
at Waterloo, closed to
passenger traffic as long
ago as 1867, but one
of the few small
branches of the
system still in use.

Aberdeen Joint station was owned by the Caledonian and G.N.oS.R. in pre-Grouping days, with running powers also held by the North British. In this view at the south end on 28 May 1930, a Deeside train is leaving, hauled by one of the earlier G.N.oS.R. 4-4-0s, No.6812.

The G.N.oS.R. operated a busy suburban service between Aberdeen and Dyce. There were a number of intermediate stations and halts served by frequent trains with smart schedules. These were however withdrawn by the L.N.E.R. in 1937 as a result of increasing tram and bus competition. The trains were worked by a fleet of nine 0-4-4Ts, one of these (No.6885) being seen near Kittybrewster in the earlier years of the Grouping.

Tillynaught, junction for the Banff branch, on 16 June 1949, with a through express from Inverness to Aberdeen, hauled by G.E.R. 4-6-0 No.61536 and B1 No.61307.

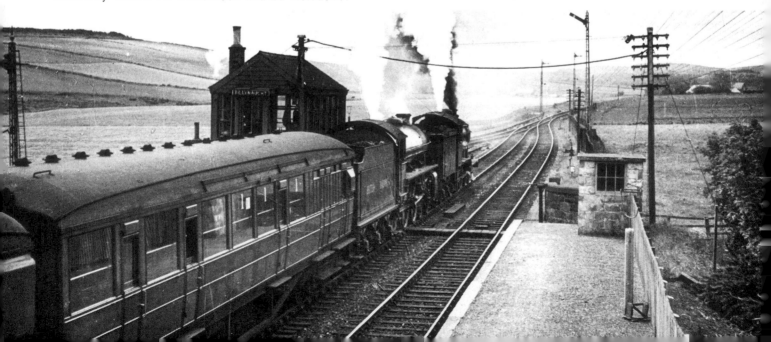

Two branches existed to the north-east coast, not quite the proverbial 'stone's throw' apart but literally within sight of one another at their termini, although separated by the River Deveron and joined only by a circuitous route of no less than 101 miles by rail. The obvious way for an enthusiast to visit both branches was to walk from one to the other. G.N.oS.R. 4-4-0 No.2256 (above) is running round its train at Banff in June 1949, whilst the lower illustration shows the terminus at Macduff on the same date. The engine is No.62277 *Gordon Highlander*, now preserved in original condition as G.N.oS.R. No.49. Macduff lost its passenger service in October 1951, followed by Banff in July 1964, both lines now being closed entirely.

Craigendoran was the start of the most spectacularly scenic route in the whole of the British Isles, the old West Highland Railway to Fort William and Mallaig. The W.H.R. was actually a separate company authorised in 1889 and opened in 1894, but was worked from the beginning by the North British, eventually to become part of the L.N.E.R. The usual provision of main line trains through to Fort William was only three or four per day, but there was also a local service as far as Arrochar and Tarbet from Craigendoran, giving connection off the trains from Glasgow to Helensburgh; however this ceased in 1964. Two of the handsome 4-4-2Ts of the N.B.R. (the only engines of their type on any Scottish railway), Nos.67460 and 67474, were latterly fitted with push-and-pull apparatus for these duties—very rare in Scotland—and the last-mentioned is seen at Craigendoran Upper on 5 July 1957. The platform of the low level line to Helensburgh can be seen in the foreground.   [R.M. Casserley]

A Fort William – Glasgow train near Craigendoran on 5 July 1957, double-headed by Black Five No.4497 piloting K2 Class 2-6-0 No.61775 *Loch Treig*.

Gresley built a set of six 2-6-0s in 1937/8, Class K4, especially for the West Highland line; No.6199 *Cameron of Locheil* taking water at Crianlarich on 18 June 1960.

60

North British 'Glen' class 4-4-0s, No.9407 *Glen Beasdale* and No.9307 *Glen Nevis* between Rannoch and Tulloch, on one of the wildest stretches of the line over Rannoch Moor, 3 August 1930. This was the class used almost exclusively on the West Highland until the advent of the 2-6-0s already mentioned, but the 'Glens' continued to work alongside the newcomers for a good many years.

Fort William shed on 14 June 1927, with Ben Nevis, the highest mountain in the British Isles, in the background. A number of G.N.R. 2-6-0s of Class K2 including No.4697 were transferred by the L.N.E.R. from the south for working over the West Highland line. The first of these arrived in 1925; later they were named after Scottish lochs in the surrounding area.

Fort William station, 24 July 1931, with 2-6-0 No.4699 waiting to depart for Mallaig. This station has recently been replaced by a modern structure on a new site further up the line and not so near the town centre.

A more recent view of Fort William showing the shed and yard, in which Class 4 No.44255 is engaged in shunting operations, 27 May 1961.   [M. Mensing]

The 4.50 p.m. to Mallaig crossing Lochy Viaduct, Fort William, 20 May 1961. The engine is No.62034, a new class of 2-6-0 of essentially L.N.E.R. design, produced by Thompson, but which did not appear until 1949. These Moguls, together with B1 4-6-0s, worked most of the West Highland trains in these later years of steam working, together with L.M.S. Black Fives and their B.R. Standard 73xxx class successors, in the final period before dieselisation.

[M. Mensing]

C.R. No.757, still in
pre-Grouping livery,
and 4-6-0 No.14607
approaching Oban with
a Sunday excursion,
12 June 1927.

The Callander & Oban route of the Caledonian was almost as spectacular in its own way as the West Highland. This view, taken on 19 May 1961, shows a freight at the wayside station of Loch Awe (closed temporarily after a landslide in 1965 and never reopened) behind Black Five No.45400. [M. Mensing]

Another view of No.14607 at Oban shed on the same day. This was one of a class of nine engines introduced in 1902, with driving wheels of 5' diameter, specially for this hilly road. They had in turn replaced an earlier series of 4-4-0s built in 1882, known as Oban Bogies, some of which lasted until 1930 on light duties on other parts of the system. Bogie engines were very desirable in view of the sharp curves on the Oban line, although, as seen in the illustration opposite, 0-6-0s were sometimes to be seen on piloting duties in the busy season.

Oban station, 18 May 1960, with the 9.30 a.m. to Glasgow leaving behind No.44795.   [M. Mensing]

The station pilot at Oban on the same day, Caledonian 0-4-4T No.55238.

[M. Mensing]

The famous pass of Killiecrankie, gateway to the Highlands, where the River Garry, the railway and the road all pass through this most picturesque wooded defile. The train, headed by Horwich 2-6-0 No.13105 piloting 'River' Class 4-6-0 No.14757, is crossing the viaduct and is about to plunge into a short tunnel beneath the photographer, then through the station and on to Blair Atholl before tackling the long ascent to the Grampians; 29 July 1931.

Dalnaspidal lies two miles short of the summit of the continuous ascent of 17 miles from Blair Atholl, much of it at gradients between 1 in 70 and 1 in 80. 0-6-4T No.15307 which had banked a train, is pausing to take water on its way back to Blair Atholl, where the small shed had an allocation of a few engines of this and other types suitable for banking duties. This view was taken on 15 May 1928.

Blair Atholl, 15 May 1928; a local train from Perth headed by Drummond 'Small Ben' No.14413 *Ben Alligan,* built at the Lochgorm works of the Highland Railway at Inverness in 1900. The two brothers, Peter and Dugald Drummond, built very similar engines on all the various railways on which they were locomotive superintendents at different times. Peter was on the Highland from 1896-1911, and on the G. & S.W.R. from 1912-1918. Dugald was perhaps the better known of the two; he started on the North British in 1875, until 1882, when he went to the Caledonian, and finally migrated south to the London & South Western from 1895 until his death in 1912.

Druimuachdar Summit, 15 May 1928; H.R. Jones goods No.17924 breasting the summit with a northbound freight. Two or three hours later—during which time the author had nothing else to contemplate but the scenery—an up freight appeared in the shape of an L.M.S. Class 4, No.4314. This was one of a batch built at the St. Rollox works of the C.R. in 1927 for use in Scotland, of which Nos.4312-4318 were allocated to the Highland.

1484 feet above sea level, Druimauchdar has always been regarded as the highest *standard gauge* summit in the British Isles, One has to make this provision in order to account for the Snowdon Mountain rack railway. Even allowing for this however, the claim was not strictly true at all times, as the Elvanfoot & Wanlockhead Railway of the Caledonian rose to a maximum of 1498 feet although this was only a branch line and in any case closed in 1939.

H.R. 'Castle' 4-6-0 No.14688 *Thurso Castle* entering Aviemore on 18 June 1927 with an express for Inverness. These engines were the mainstay of main line working over the Highland for many years after the introduction in 1900 and were constructed in small batches until 1917.

On the same occasion as mentioned on page 74, it had been a lucky break to obtain a ride on the footplate from a friendly driver on 'Loch' Class No.14393 *Loch Laochal* from Dalnaspidal to the summit; this engine is seen here amongst the magnificent Grampian mountain scenery, before returning to Aviemore, from whence it had piloted an up train.

Gollanfield, junction for the Fort George branch on 21 July 1931. 'River' Class 4-6-0 No.14759, one of built in 1915 for the Highland Railway but found too heavy by the engineers' department and tak over by the Caledonian. After the Grouping they were able to be transferred back to the line for which th were originally built. The branch train is in the charge of No.14398 *Ben Alder*, eventually set aside for servation, a project which unfortunately did not materialise.

A scene on another of the Highland's several branches, Fochabers, on 26 May 1930. Former main line engines frequently worked out their declining years on such duties and it was the custom to turn the engine round for each trip, even on the shorter branches, to avoid tender-first running. No.14274 *Strathcarron* was one of the last survivors of a very fine batch of twelve 4-4-0s, built by Neilson & Co. in 1892, relegated after many years of express working to more humble duties.

Over the years numerous photographs have been taken of the former roundhouse shed at Inverness now complete demolished. This rather unusual view, taken on 19 July 1931, also well illustrates the unique louvred chimney found many Highland engines constructed by David Jones between 1869 and 1896. This one was 4-4-0T No.15010.

One of Jones' well-known 4-6-0s built in 1894, the first engines of this type in the British Isles, making a vigorous st from Inverness bound for the far north on 26 May 1930.

78

The beautiful Kyle of Lochalsh line, similar in many respects to the Oban line, also needed engines with a suitable wheelbase to cope with the sharp curves of the route, and thus were evolved the 'Skye Bogies', a series of eight 4-4-0s, built at intervals between 1882 and 1901. No.14283, bound for the Kyle, passes an up train at Achnashellach on 20 June 1927.

No.14277, the first of the Skye Bogies, working the branch train to Fortrose, photographed at Muir of Ord on 21 May 1928.

Garve, on the Kyle of Lochalsh branch, 18 June 1937; trains passing, 'Clan' goods No.17956, and Jones goods No. 17930, approaching on a local pick up goods.

The 'Clan goods', eight engines built in 1917-1919, a smaller wheeled version of the express class (the last new engines built for the Highland) were largely used on the Kyle road until 1952, when they were displaced by L.M.S. Black Fives. No.57956 at the Kyle of Lochalsh on 22 April 1952 is believed to have been the last passenger working of one of these engines, having been provided by special request to work the 5.35 p.m. train to Inverness for the benefit of a party of members of the Stephenson Locomotive Society.

[R.M. Casserley]

y the shores of Loch Carron, another very scenic section of the Kyle road, behind No.57956 on 22 April 1952.

On the 'Far North' road – Inverness to Wick and Thurso – with a train entering The Mound Junction on 19 May 1928. No.14676 *Ballindalloch Castle* is in charge.

The Mound was the junction for the Dornoch branch, The train is seen here running into the former on 23 April 195[ ] with 0-4-4T No.55051. Together with its sister 55053, this was the last Highland engine to remain in traffic, bei[ ] withdrawn in June 1956 and January 1957 respectively. They were replaced on this service by a couple of G.W.[ ] type pannier tanks. The Dornoch branch was closed in June 1960, and like all other Highland branches, ne[ ] succumbed to the use of diesel railcars.

84   Another view of No.55051 at The Mound on 23 April 1952. Only the stone piers of the viaduct now remain[ ]

Stanier 'Black Five' No.45479 on an up train near Helmsdale, on 15 June 1949, amongst typical scenery on the Far North Road.

Typical Highland station on the Far North Road—Kildonan, with a north bound train hauled by Class 5s Nos.45476 and 45124, 23 April 1952.

Georgemas Junction, the most northerly in the British Isles. The same train as depicted above heading for Wick, after having detached the rear portion for Thurso. This will be taken on by *Ben Alder*, standing at the up main line platform, which will work tender first to Britain's most northerly railhead, 23 April 1952. The same procedure exists today, but of course operated by diesel locomotives.

An up Highland express near Slochd summit, 20 July 1931. Ten of these Horwich 2-6-0s, later known as 'Crabs', built at Crewe in 1928-9, Nos.13100-13109 (later 2800-2809) were sent north to the Highland and quickly established themselves as being capable of working the heaviest express trains alongside the 'Clans' and the ageing 'Castles', which they to some extent superseded. They were eventually replaced in their turn by L.M.S. Black 5s.

The early 1960s were golden years for the enthusiast, when it was possible for Societies to arrange rail tours over various interesting and unusual lines in Scotland, many of them not normally used by passenger trains. Some of these made use of the four engines restored to pre-Grouping condition in full working order, through the enterprise of Scottish Region, This view, taken at Dalwhinnie on 15 June 1960, where the Highland Jones goods is pausing to take water, was on a seven day tour organised jointly by the Stephenson Locomotive Society and the Railway Correspondence & Travel Society, covering many of Scotland's most scenic routes. [R.M. Casserley]

This view, taken on 20 April 1962, was the occasion of a Branch Line Society special consisting of the Caledonian single and two Caledonian Railway coaches, seen here at Ayr.

[Derek Cross]

The North British 4-4-0 No.256 *Glen Douglas*, between Ladybank and Newburgh, with a Railway Correspondence & Travel Society special on 28 August 1965. This was *Glen Douglas's* last steam outing.

[Derek Cross]

Great North of Scotland Railway *Gordon Highlander* with Highland Railway Jones goods No.103 running light through Barrhill on 13 April 1963 on their way to Stranraer to work a special on the following Monday. All four of these preserved engines were placed in Glasgow Museum, where they now rest, after the official ban placed on steam working, since to some extent relaxed. [Derek Cross]

The sad end of steam, typified here by B1 No.61243 hauling withdrawn Caledonian 0-6-0s Nos.57262, 57392 and 57362 away from Ayr for scrap, passing Falkland Junction on 22 April 1963.   [Derek Cross]

Another view of condemned engines en route from Carlisle to the West of Scotland Ship Breaking Company at Troon; Black Five No.44955 hauling rebuilt 'Scot' No.46155 *The Lancer* and rebuilt 'Patriot' No.45527 *Southport* near Auchinleck, 10 March 1965.

[Derek Cross]

All steam in Scotland was officially withdrawn as from 1 January 1967, but nonetheless NB J36 No.65345 was still shunting happily at Seafield Colliery three months later. A week after this photograph was taken on 25 March 1967 'authority' heard of it, and the practice ceased forthwith—and this was the final regular B.R. steam working in Scotland. How strange that this last duty was carried out by a humdrum pre-Grouping veteran dating back to 1900!

[Derek Cross]